Tributes

Other Carcanet titles by Elizabeth Jennings

Collected Poems
(W.H. Smith Book Award, 1987)
Selected Poems
Growing Points
Consequently I Rejoice
Moments of Grace
Extending the Territory
Celebrations and Elegies

ELIZABETH JENNINGS

Tributes

CARCANET

For Cotty

Acknowledgements are due to the editors of the following magazines in which some of these poems first appeared: *Agenda, Aquila, Critical Quarterly, Encounter, London Magazine, New Blackfriars, PN Review, Poetry Review, Rialto, Spectator* and *The Tablet*. The "Tate Gallery" sequence was commissioned by the Tate Gallery, London.

First published in 1989 by
Carcanet Press Limited
208-212 Corn Exchange
Manchester M4 3BQ

British Library Cataloguing in Publication Data

Jennings, Elizabeth 1926-
    Tributes.
    I. Title
    821'.914

    ISBN 0 85635 756 1

The publisher acknowledges the financial assistance of
the Arts Council of Great Britain.

Typeset in 10pt Palatino by Bryan Williamson, Manchester
Printed in England by SRP Ltd, Exeter

Contents

Tributes	9
For George Herbert	10
Notes to *The Winter's Tale*	11
For Charles Causley	12
For Philip Larkin	13
Tribute to Turner	15
Caravaggio	16
Goya	17
Chardin	18
After a Painting is Finished	19
Tate Gallery (I, II)	21
The Arts	23
A Roman Trio	24
Sant' Anselmo on the Aventine Hill, Rome	24
Ostia Antica	25
Lake Albano outside Rome	25
Spain	27
Once in Greece	28
Anzio	30
The Gulf of Salerno	31
Some Words of my Mother's in Childhood	32
Fairground	33
Psalm of Childhood	34
Psalm of Discrepancies	35
By Themselves	36
Spring and a Blackbird	37
True Spring	38
Dusk	39
Cloudscape	40
Moon in December	41
Newcomer	42
Aubade	43
A Music Sought	44
Arrival and Preparation	45
Enough	46
Two Together	47
At the Source	48
Always	49

Presences   51
Friendship   52
Total   54
Landscape and Wild Gardens   55
Winter Piece   56
In Such Slow Sweetness   57
For Melody   58
Two Musics   59
All that Departing   60
A Living Death   62
Time for the Elegy   64
Gone   65
The Spirit Lifts   66
One Minute   67
Young Love   68
The Feel of Things   69
Some Solitude   70
Fifteen Years after a Death   71
Legacies and Language   72
The House of Words   74
The Early Work   75
Think of   76
Art and Time   77
Pigeons Suddenly   78
The Luck of it   79
The Start of a Story   80
Against the Dark   81
The Sea as Metaphor   82
I Heard a Voice   83
Parts   85
Let it be   86
Waiting   87
The Prodigal Son   89
The Hours   90
Saint Augustine   91
For Easter 1986   92
Easter Vigil and Mass   93
Gloria   94
In Good Time   95
A Reproach   96
Moving Together   97

Only	98
Snooker	99
Group Life	100
First Six Years	101
A Childhood Religion	103
The Essential	104
Talking of Hume	105
Thinking of Descartes	106
The Force of Time	108
Of Time	110
Distractions	112
There is Time	113
Passion	114
Mastery	115
Energy	116
Turning Inland	117
Resolve	118
On the Edge of My Mind	119
Justice	120
Question	121
Nocturne	122
A Happy Death	123
Beginning	128

A Letter of Thanks
(For Cotty)

In your handsome house where everything eases the eye
    And young and old are one
Since in your thoughts age is forgotten, I
Am happy and grateful. Warm April lies upon

Delicate willows and all the air is in bloom
    But most of yesterday was
Destruction and argument. Broken a little I come
Into your magic circle which means pure grace.

I am learning wisdom from you every day,
    Each hour. You walk through my mind
And set the images dancing, the words to play,
You opened my eyes again when I was blind

With ludicrous tears of hurt, but to you they meant
    Somebody needed your heart,
Your sweet goodwill. Love is your one element
In which you let me share. I am a part

Of the family of uncountable ones you know
    And care about. You are
As welcoming as this lavish April, also
For me in my lucky sky a new-found star.

Tributes

Debts can be burdens and can lead to hate
But there are others which are strong in love
And lift us into a harmonious state,

Judicious, full, compassionate. They move
Us into joys we'd never dreamt about,
Seldom thought possible. I've learnt enough

Of the heart's follies and of serious doubt
To question what the senses claim, I've found
In recent years a warmth which pulls me out

Of lassitude, indifference. Around
The long shelves of my mind I've come upon
Writers, painters, mystics who abound

In gifts my poems have reflected on
And whom I wish to sing and celebrate.
It is not only great stars or the sun

I owe so many debts to. I now state
A poet here, a painter there, a place
That's altered all I do. So I relate

My debts and give back what I've taken, grace.

For George Herbert

You'd understand the gratitude I feel,
  My need to tell it too.
Sometimes in great love someone wants to kneel
  In reverence, and you
Would understand the tears and joy of this.
I've learnt of trust and hope from you. It is

More than a pleasure, passion shakes the sense
  And glows within the mind.
When I've been low I've felt your deference
  To all that dogs mankind
And all that also gives him happiness.
It is within your words. Your emphasis

Is on the drama lived in each man's soul,
  His battle with his flawed
Aspirations and you make him whole
  Telling of his Lord
Who battled too though God in every pore
And pity. No-one wrote like this before.

You loved the monosyllable and it
  Runs through your music. I
Can hear between its graces music yet
  More deep and much more high.
You have released my spirit, sent it on
Audacious flights by what you've said and done.

Notes to "The Winter's Tale"

We knew it in childhood, always found it in
Garden or park. When we chased birds we were
Small spirits of this Summer harbinger
When we made Daisy-Chains they were for her
This is how all Persephones begin.

Within the minds of children most myths start
And this assuredly is one of such.
Spring is in the child's pulse. Its heart
Beats in response to this Corn Goddess's touch.
At harvest no-one can resist so much
Abundance, yet there has to be some hurt,
Some offering and here it is field-mice
Whose huddled horror is the sacrifice.

For Charles Causley

Cornwall is your pasture and your pleasure,
The granite cliffs, the high sea, and each cove
The sea rides into puts us at our leisure

For we are tourists. We know little of
The spell of that long sweep of England where
You've lived so long that Cornwall is a love

You'll never lose. In bracing, salty air,
In high white horses all the year round, you
Have now become a part of all that's there.

The open and the secret places know
Your step and gaze. So now I praise a place
And doing so I offer thanks to you

For all your poetry and its lyric grace
Which are so rare now. You have taught me much
About the need to work upon my verse.

I see you seldom yet I feel in touch.

For Philip Larkin

I

The last thing you would have wanted –
A poem in praise of you. You would have smiled,
Cracked a joke and then gone back into
Your secret self, the self that exposed itself
To believe in nothing after death, to a trust
In traditional customs, marriage, falling in love
And behaving with kindness and courtesy. You watched
Horses put out to grass,
The wonder of Queen Anne's lace,
To everything English and green and bound by rivers,
The North with its dark canals:
I see you suddenly caught by a brilliant moon
In the early hours. I offer you words of praise
From these time-rent, beleaguered
Violent void-of-you days.

II

English faces, private, hiding away
Hurt or love gone wrong, the stubborn waste
Of meadows built on. Every end of day

Must have seemed to you, as it does to me, the last
Since we threaten to break the planet now. I see
Your watchful care over the chosen past.

Once you said that poetry was a way
To preserve, enshrine, and to give purpose to all
That seems more senseless and furious every day.

You are a distance away and yet in call
As I turn your pages over. *The Less Deceived*
Delights me most of all your books. I feel

That *Wedding Wind*. Here are all you believed
In always – the gentle touch, the tender care
For the long-dead poor. I always feel relieved

And less afraid when I read what you would share.

13

III

Was your silence the quiet of desperation?
Did you feel wholly helpless when you saw
The ruined future beyond your explanation?
Or was there in your heart a private war?
Perhaps your isolation

From passion, disorder felt to you like regret,
As if you had made the wrong decision, a choice
Not to opt out but to stand aside and let
Discord or harmony happen. We miss your voice.
The very quiet of it

Often consoled us and yet there is a lack
In your later poems. It seems as if you saw
Your failed past and wanted to have it back
And choose again. But in your verse a law
Is clear, you refused to speak

When there was nothing to say. You hated all
That Modernism meant and yet your verse
Sings of now and here. We hear its call
As the future assaults and every day grows worse
With vice and war. Was a wall

Built up deliberately by you? Did you hide
From the greater issues? No, your silence was
Imperative and resonant. You died
In a dark Winter leaving all of us
Needing you at our side.

Tribute to Turner

(A sonnet)

What were your bonds and limits? It is hard
For us to see them yet there must be some
Since art can only flourish locked and barred
By form. However inward; it must come

To keep off sprawl and chaos. Out of sight
Yours are but they are firm. Within your craft
The storm, the tides are held by day and night,
Leashed strongly in and so the looker's left

With fire and flood and steam. There is no fear
For us but only wonder. Nature is
At your command when you most disappear

And so we're caught up in your ecstasies
And large delight that's present everywhere
And what seems peril has the power to please.

Caravaggio

It wasn't violence I noticed first,
Your *Narcissus* took me by surprise,
The polished light, the pair of eyes that trust
Those repeated. I knew that my eyes
Were wiped of usual dust

And I was shown again how light is proud
And threatening and will not be denied
To one like you who took pimps from a crowd,
Put them in poses for a God who'd died.
Brutal you were, not crude.

And accurate, impatient of mere sketching.
The rounds and squares of suffering you made
Arresting, overmastering, overreaching.
Christ Entombed was how the rich light played,
The spirit drifting, touching.

Goya

It is a kind of force which does not touch
The sadist nerve, the calculating thought.
Here is the soul at work within the rich
Muscle and sinew. Goya always caught
That vigour out of reach

To lesser painters who make violence
A proper end. We do not look for long
Unless we are the few who love the sense
Of hurt that does not hurt us. Here the strong
Purpose is intense

And tense also and draws our admiration,
When war's the issue we are shown the loss
Of spirit and are taught that satisfaction
Of our brute senses points the worst in us
While the true connection

Of flesh and spirit is united by
Goya's pure vision. Portraits by him show
A man alert and eager. We see why
Unity governs clearer than we know
When Goya lends his eye.

Chardin

Is it the lack of self that most of all
    Challenges eyes to stay
And linger over the petals that will not fall
    Although they have some way

Of suggesting that Chardin, had he wanted to, could
    Have moved the steady light?
Here is still-life that tells us Nature is good,
    Here is a seize of sight.

After a Painting is Finished
(For Alec Guinness)

He is hunched against a wall
And his hands cover his eyes, his feet fit together.
If you draw close you will hear him murmuring, not
To you but to himself, and what he is saying
Is "That is not what I meant."
What he did not mean is a canvas on an easel
Still wet but finished. The painter is almost in tears,
The picture is full of light and people walking.
It is a city scene on a gala day.
Flags are flying, rosettes

Are worn by men, and the children
Hold the strings of silver, heart-shaped balloons,
The scene is sharing merriment and more,
More which is hard to put into words. Is the painter
Feeling this? To us the scene's a success.

Nothing is overstated,
Much is left to imagination and we
Want to free that along the streets, in the sky.
A fiesta, a feast day is part of a special vision,
The moon is full and could not be anything else.
Why does the painter appear

So desolate, so sad, so disappointed?
What did he mean that we do not recognise?
Does every work of art leave the maker feeling
His work is unfinished and the failure is his own?
This painter is now shedding tears.

We dare not approach him and we do not need
To ask, as with some abstract paintings, exactly
What every symbol means. Simplicity
Is the hallmark of the canvas on his easel
And we are pleased to look.

But maybe we should call to mind that when we
Say, bake a cake, embroider a cloth, or sing
A snatch of song, we are often dissatisfied.
Are these on a lower level than what's shown here?
We do not know. We only feel compassion.

This man feels sure that he has not portrayed
The vision held in his mind, that he's let something down
Or disappointed others as well as himself.
Maybe in a Garden of Eden a painting
Would be a perfect work of art, and yet

Surely Adam and Eve did not need to make
Works of art. Their visions stood all around them,
The sun was supremely itself, the trees exactly
What their creator intended and so were all the flowers
And birds and beasts. There did not have to be art

Made by man in his once perfect state,
And there is much to prove that we have fallen
From grace and integrity. Every work of art
Then, it appears, must be approximate only,
The maker has quickly lost interest in what he made

And doubtless this man will get up and look about him,
Take down the canvas and put its face to the wall,
Pick out a clean one, and squeeze new paint on his palette,
Feeling zest rise in him, hope that indeed one day
He will please himself as he has pleased his viewers.

But it seems more likely he'll soon be squatting once more
Against a gate or wall and will be saying
"That picture isn't what I saw in my mind,
My imagination held a great comprehension,
A world of new life and colour." He'll never stop
Painting if he's an honest maker. How odd
That we should see completion where he sees part,
For he is, in little, a God.

Tate Gallery

I

Think of these at night when no-one sees
The fearful summons and unsparing brush,
Ernst is a hunter with dark images.

Imagine ghosts of gazers seeing flesh
Hinted at. Rodin is there of course,
Yet in a night-time gallery, the wish

Of all past lookers and their live discourse
Might haunt the air. "Here" one might say, "My dread
Is captured. I've had dreams like that, a curse

On easy sleeping". Do these painters then
Darken our day to help us through the night
Knowing that we are scared and little men?

Perhaps, but we are ones who climb to bright
Precarious moments, love those abstract lines
Of Nicholson and Mondrian. Our sight

Is sharpened in this place of many signs
Directing us within but also out
To how the sky behaves or moon reclines.

The Tate's purpose cannot be in doubt.

II

Place of mirror and mirage, hint, retirement and then
Sudden fierce arrivals after shunting in sidings of paintings which
    have unloaded
Influence, bias and bring in their own views of now, visions of
    time beyond us almost, also
Warhol, Pollock, Hockney, all, in a way, shockers, shapers of work
Which affronts us, takes us by the scruff, giddys us to come round
    and stand, shakily still
Before the risk and rise of intemperate choices, blatant colours,
    bearers

Almost of ungrace. And yet, and yet. . . . look closer,
Dare to stare at the tricks played by Magritte, be willing to admit
The painters had to leap down unconscious minds, and
Out-Freud Freud, healing not by talking trouble away, but by
    being forced
To admit art must go this way, find a difficult sturdy beauty in
    all unlikeliness.
And, as a touchstone, stare at Blake or Palmer.
Open your eyes to your own mind reflected
But improved, given form and purpose,
Painted out of the colour-box of the rainbow,
Shocking us only to save us for this moment
In an age at ease with violence and terror.
An almost impossible peace may here be gathered,
But has to be won by a courage of total looking.

The Arts

Only lately have I
Questioned the nub of verse
Sought in the heart's cry
The purpose of art to us

And the more I reflect the less
Do I seem to understand.
Music can always bless
While under the sculptor's hand

Abstract shapes convey
The mind ill at ease with the heart.
What poets have to say
Was difficult from the start,

Twisted language played games
With meaning and metaphor.
I write when the craft claims
What I never knew before.

A Roman Trio

No other place so holy,
No other hill so resonant and calm
So utterly itself. I learnt of it
When someone said "The best singing in Rome
Is at the Sunday Mass at Sant' Anselmo,
The mother house of all the Benedictines"
I found an early bus and got off at
The Aventine's still base. I was alone
And early for the Mass. I walked up slowly
And on my right found St. Dominic's church,
Santa Sabina, carefully restored,
Soft-stoned and simple, no mosaics or frescoes,
Near the entrance a carved wooden door
Shaped before St. Dominic was born.
No-one was there. I knew I would return
Often, I knew this was my special hill
Among Rome's seven. Soon Mass would begin
And so I moved on to the hill's peak and
Entered the Benedictine church. Of course,
Nuns were already in the front row but
I did not care. Soon ninety monks assembled,
Lastly the Abbot. Latin Mass began,
The universal language of the church,
The tongue familiar since my childhood but
I'd never heard music like this before,
Such lofty voices, masculine and clear,
And magisterial – *Credo, Gloria* and
Sanctus. I had never known till then,
Felt and thought, such sure serenity,
Bread into Christ, wine to his blood, and time
Existed only in the Rome of squares
And shops and fountains. I came out of Mass
And wandered down the hill between the roses
Turning their faces to me, early June
Faces of pink and red and white. I carried
The singing of the Benedictines in
My spirit as I entered central Rome,
All of me deepened, sharpened, happy too.

II. *Ostia Antica*

We were out of Rome,
Out of the dust and heat of it,
Even the heat of early June was clasping hot fingers
Round ruin, church, fountain. Over each hill hung
A veil of mist, but we were out of this,
Walking knee-deep in thick grass like English grass
And through English flowers with their clear translucent names,
Bird's Eye, Shepherd's Purse, Queen Anne's Lace and Buttercups,
And the various grasses, some cutting, some soothing,
Rose up from the black-and-white mosaics insisting we look
At elephant, horse, fishes, snakes. St Augustine's name
Hung in the air too till we brought it down
Into our voices, talked of the City of God
Not, after all, far off.
But time was measured only now by our shadows
And the ripe blue sky and the noon dome of the sky,
And we spoke as if words were plucked out of the air
Or out of the earth, or both
And it seemed not impossible echoes still drifted here,
Augustine and Monica talking,
Voices rooted among the grass and the buttercups
And the sky going suddenly dark as we would not see it.
Didn't we speak very low?
Didn't we almost whisper
As if otherwise we might drown out the living echoes
Or stir two saints from sleep?

III. *Lake Albano Outside Rome*

Associated with Autumn always,
Lake Albano seems made for it. That day
After a good lunch, with Rome still almost in sight,
The sky pale blue, we trod on the crisp bronze leaves,
Talking of history, saints and visionaries,
Sometimes not speaking at all
For that air begged quiet and we were acquiescent
With this good silence. Now and then a bird
Far out of sight, sang the snatch of a song.
There was the lake so still, dark brown,
Darker than leaves. An image of eternity,

I thought, but did not say.
On we went walking steadily, not specially fast
For time seemed a string we wound up as we progressed,
A silken string left by the Summer. That walk
Is with me now in an English record-cold Winter
And you, my good friend, who opened your private map
Of Rome and shared it with me, have been dead seven years.
Thirty years ago we met, you a holy man,
Myself an eager young poet, in love with Rome,
Heart-free in all other ways. Heart-breaks were over
For those three months and I only realize now
How open I was to a city made half of light
And half of the world's power. I loved it gently, carefully,
Let it take me by strong hand and heart slowly. I met
So much kindness from simple Italians and some
English priests and poets. It was as if
An unhappy childhood was handed back and altered,
An illuminated spell cast round me and on me
During so many days and nights. Now this was October,
My first in Rome. I had been there in Spring and Summer
Until the big heat. We had finished our circular walk and were
        talking again,
Then catching a bus back to Rome, a city with arms
Open to me then and always, a mother, the world's true centre
Awaiting me now as I meditate on a return.

Spain

I have written so little about it, in truth
Hardly a word. It was Rome, Rome
On my mind always, and when I saw even a single
Cypress only on a dusty path I thought
Always of Italy.

I went to Spain often enough,
One month in each year for was it.....
Five years? I remember siestas when I
Worked and you slept. Now and then
I too was captured by sleep.

But I would not try hard with that tongue,
Harsher than Italy's, louder, unrelenting, then
Loud in "Oles". There would never be bullfights, never
In all of Italy.

Italians can be brutal but quietly. Spain
Spoke of the fiery spirit, prayer rising
From John in his tower, from Teresa
Enclosed in her Avila.

I often missed the laughter of Rome, the shameless
Shows of feeling, the lack of dignity. Spain
Was what I admired, never what I might love.
I look down at the map,

At that square of Europe, vast peninsula, think
Of Goya and energy, El Greco and Christ but still
Rome draws my spirit. Campaniles are hers
And so are squares and prayers and absolving words.
Spain was a cold, pure passion.

Once in Greece

The Sirens sang in childhood, islands shone
With strong sun I had never seen in England.
This was imagination mapping out

Later voyages. How right they were
To speak of "Greece and Rome" since in most ways
Rome is indeed the whole of Italy,

More than a city anyway. Was this
Why Athens disappointed me? Had I
Shaped too many islands, set the sun

Too richly on the sea? It may be so.
Athens was noise and Babel. No-one spoke
My French or English, and of course I was

Often consciously comparing this
Noisy city with the stretch of Rome.
Its blend of luxury and abstinence,
Its run of hills, its history carried lightly,
A place of arts, tradition and of conquest.
At least I learnt, though, Athens was not Greece.

My mind unburdened it upon that trip
In golden May to Corinth and Mycenae,
But there the sickness started and I saw
Epidaurus through a yellow mist,
Felt far too weak to test the vast acoustics
And yet the resin smell of that slow walk

Towards the theatre lingers in my nostrils
With the dark sea I had one long warm swim in
And yet I felt a stranger all the time

In Athens, specially with the English there;
Stubborn imagination of my childhood
Kept on comparing its huge dream with this
Wide range of mauve hills. Here the gods were dead
And even road-side shrines for Jesus Christ
Had an uncertain and a fragile air.

Maybe I never caught the music of
Greece. All countries have an undertone
Of rhythm caught on winds and rising voices,

Sounds that never finish, flutes which play
For the old times when Dryads grew in trees.
Rome kept intruding and I felt its sway,

Its subtle rhythms, hidden melodies
Held in my heart when Greece lay all around
But would not yield the past in one pure sound.

Anzio

(In memory of A. T.-A.)

We went for lunch at a hotel kept by a friend
Of this friend who took me to Anzio. The day
Was cool and easy. The sky
Pale with a Roman blue, a Spring blue still.
After lunch we sat with coffee and strega
(Sticky and sweet but it tastes of Rome to me)
And looked at the idle fishing boats at anchor.
The barely visible lap of the sea, the beach
Deserted. We fell into a reverie
Each allowed the other and after an hour –
Anzio still in siesta sleep about us –
You suddenly said you wanted to see the graves
Of the Protestant soldiers killed in the Second World War.
Then I remembered you'd fought in the First World War,
First in the trenches, then in a fragile plane.
You clearly needed to go
Partly to pay your homage, partly to leave
The beach once invaded by British soldiers, their blood
In your imagination all about you.
So we took a carozza in sweet slow afternoon
And dawdled among the graves. That invasion, those deaths
Meant nothing to me. My war had been hunger simply
Felt in a very "safe area", but through
Your eyes I saw two wars, soldiers in trenches,
Others running on sand amid noise of guns
And the afternoon was broken. Our silences
Floating over these graves were a drift of fear,
Of wounds and death, and now you were a priest
Daily giving the sacraments and changing
Wine into Blood. Is it whimsical to
Remember the pink sky later that afternoon
And see it as blood till the Mediterranean night
Dropped its kind folds about us and we went back
From the echoes of war and the idle fishing boats
To Rome your home and swiftly becoming mine.

The Gulf of Salerno

The Bay of Naples paled as we rounded the corner,
The bus driver singing snatches of *Rigoletto*
And spinning the driving wheel with a single hand,
His reckless joy imparted itself to us,
Such infectious delight. The bright sky echoed with sounds
Of a recitative. Then suddenly all noise stopped
Or so it seemed. Maybe imagination
Was playing a rôle, but no, there was indeed
No need of anything but this natural grandeur
Of that still bay: spears of stone stood up
And to our left were towns like limpets clinging
To the sheer cliff. At Positano we stopped
And admired the lace a smiling old lady was making.
I had seen her copy in Rome, the same shrewd eyes,
The sunburnt and wrinkled skin. She did not mind
That we looked but did not buy. Our smiles were enough.
Back in the bus we hurried along to Amalfi
Almost silent, nothing of tragedy there
Though echoes of Webster's *Duchess* spoke in my mind
But only briefly. Full noon held us within
Its huge hot bubble of air. Once more we stopped
And ate our rolls and cheese in a cypress shadow.
The driver lay under the sun with his cap
Over his face. Siesta was everywhere,
The dark, still water had made its peace with the sky.

Some Words of My Mother's in Childhood

When I was a child I never said "When I shall die"
Or "When my life ends." I didn't believe in death
Or ends. This made for great joy and huge fear.
I believed that the happy ride on the carousel
Would never end and in a sense it did not
For when I was lifted off the horse or the dragon
I was riding still, hugging the animals' sides
And falling asleep to the hurdy-gurdy music.

But when I had been afraid of a saint in a chapel
Of a huge cathedral because a white handkerchief covered
His face, I cried and screamed in bed that night
Because my imagination was schooled to mysteries,
To holding back, to being open to wonder
And so my fear was an overmastering presence
Larger than full moon or the tumbling clouds
Or the blowing trees. Somebody strong had to speak
And break the evil spell and so you did,
My gentle mother. You somehow stilled the sobbing
And carefully drew from my gasping words the story
Of the saint who was dead and whose face I could not see.
You said – and such magic there was of rich assurance
In your quiet voice – "He's laughing at you in Heaven"
The room became small, the wind was friendly, the moon
A face nodding with wise approval at me.
Let me be grateful always for the power
Of casting out devils of fear from a child of six
Let me learn how to help those frightened others
Who have no words but look to me for meaning
Or who write and say they often read my poems,
May my music be selfless and pure as my mother's sentence
Which soothed the child I am though now a poet
For I've lost nothing of fear or horror but only
Been given the magic charms of poems which drive
Out the devils that darken love. Let those fraught figments
In others' minds change to a rich peace
When my poems arm them and take them over and soften
However briefly the dreadful disturbance of life.

32

Fairground

(In memory of my Father)

There it was, Big Dipper, Giant Racer, Figure of Eight,
Any name, a fairground near the sea
And I was five years old jumping and shouting and begging you
    to take me
High up there into the clouds and the sun. You paused at first
And then went up to test the ride without me. I watched you go
Out of my sight, heard the engine pounding, saw the steep
Climb and the dips and I was all excitement, elation and when
    you came
Out of the glory of golden air you picked me up,
Put me between your knees and slowly we climbed
Up the sheerest slope I'd ever seen or felt
And I was afraid but joyfully so, you held me tight
Between your knees, your hands over mine and how could I know
This was the closest we'd ever be, that never again
Would there be a ride to the Heavens, you bearing me up
And me all trust and delight? The engine dipped
Down and up and down again with the élan of speed and the air
Ran through our hair, time was somewhere else
Until we began to slow and came down at last
To the usual world of flatness but I was still
Up with the sun and you holding me tight
In a closeness so sweet, in a timeless pleasure of height.

Psalm of Childhood

I was near it, close to the world around me seeming within me
And glad to be there. The psalm of a child, the singing, the glory,
　　the terror
Are like the majestic psalms sung in Office, telling the world its
　　trouble,
How the bones sing, are broken, how God is terrible too but
　　somehow loving.
Listen, I looked at the sparrow and robin and starling,
Watched their immediate hold on the world, their assurance
Obvious in all their singing and arguing, sure that they were
　　always essential and needed
As the Great Bear is and the Southern Cross and the moon's
　　discreet alterations.
Children are adept and swift at praise undivided
From the lion's wild ways to the zebra's astonishment at
Its audacious stripes that it can never hide.
I lay in the humming grass or hay, I hid among shrubs and
　　hedgerows
And smelt the rain on the wind and plucked the vetch and
　　convolvulus
And saw its shrinking with tears.
I rejoiced in the swelling apples, the hairy gooseberry, the black-
　　berries and their juice,
And I watched the horizon swallowing sunlight but leaving
Such a spread and depth and so many shapes and shades
Of red and pink and purple.
And make no mistake, I know that I am still
As rich and wild in my ways but also tempered
By love gone wrong or betrayed or altered or darkened.
I drew cool shadows in childhood little knowing
They would stand around me later and close me in
And so they do but I cry from the depths of their reaching
With praise and presumptuous defiance and trust and need
And sometimes the world answers back.

Psalm of Discrepancies

When did I first sing to the clouds of rejection
Turn to the fertile fields with a fiery mind,
Set my imagination in tune with storms
Or the wake of storms? I do not know. I know
Only the stretches of memory, the Alps
Of recollection, Himalayas of hope.
Childhood is almost a psalm in itself or a set
Of psalms with their moods of anger and desolation
And hope and imploring. David's language sings me
Back to the shapes of childhood, its squares and oblongs,
Its definite colours. I called to the green fields often
Ran through the dew of early morning and gathered
Nosegays and branches for gifts. They were mementoes
For later years, talismans for the ways
No longer straight or certain when clouds are smoky and hide
That joy which swelled beyond my containment, dispersed
Among the green branches of oak and ash and beech.
So I was lost in a world of drama but seldom
Felt lonely or frightened. Never by day I mean,
Never in any resplendent noon. So now
When I am troubled and angry or half-way-between
I turn the pages back in an ancient *Book
Of Certain Hours* and find my childhood markers
Between the pages and all the past is renewed
And dazzles me with the sunrise upon green hills
And sunset over a sea which is not tidal.

By Themselves

I give the clouds a revelry of song,
Blow them up with trumpets till they float
Like white balloons about the preening sun.
I let go all of Summer but it's caught

And tied up in my mind with other years,
Childhood content when sun shone every day,
I lost myself among those cavaliers
Of lancing light. As music plays I play

Today and consciously set self aside.
The barley's burnt and ready for the gather
When we are needed. Threshing floors are wide.
We are citizens whose town is weather,

And always we press our imaginings
Upon the ripe and unripe fruit. I try
To offer liberation to all things,
Accept that I can't change worlds with my eye.

Music with no voices is the one
Sound we make that does not sing of us.
I listen to a cello, it's begun
Pure cadences that we cannot abuse.

Spring and a Blackbird

Today words have a tune.
Who found which? Who knows
Which came first? The singing goes
Up and up in swinging circles, in sound
Where intimate conversation never goes.
A poem takes off from the ground,
From snow safe and from heat-wave it's immune,
Part-sunlight, part-half-moon.

And the sound of the poem belongs
To nobody. It's a free for all,
A high clarity like the blackbird's call
In this green-gold morning, this burning afternoon.
You need not search for music in your poems,
You, poet. They find each other out
Plangent, intransigent and never in doubt
As the blackbird is, and not becomes its tune.

True Spring

Is it true Spring, this rush of light into
A sky long shrouded in a Winter dark?
I smell fresh atmosphere, I count each blue

Circle or square of sky. In every park
Purple and yellow crocuses abound
In their squat brilliance. I feel something quick

Upon my skin, and in my mind a sound
Of blackbirds calling lifts my spirit and
I am content to stand on this green ground.

I am content to watch the birds descend
On softening soil. I feel a part of Spring.
Persephone now takes me by the hand

And at her bidding thrushes start to sing.

Dusk

Is dusk the favourite hour for many people?
The English gradual change of light I mean,
The slow, soft shadows filling out, the sky

Bonfired and well-augured when it's red
(That's a saw I've never known to fail).
Dusk is precious, even when it's long

And lingers as if eager to stay with us,
Cruising shadows round rich Summer trees,
Lengthening stems of Spring flowers, stealthy movements:

It is a time of many mixed-up feelings,
Almost contradictions which link hands.
Now I think of Southern sudden nights

When there's no dusk at all, no Western red
And pink but sudden plunges into dark
The happiest time for me, these falls in Rome

For then it is as if a huge hand pinned
Brooches of stars upon the Southern heights
Of sky. The Southern Cross is diamonds for

A mythic god or king, a cause for myths.
I love the South but I love English dusks,
The subtle twilight, most things juxtaposed,

Shadow and substance, pale moon facing sun,
Stars like splinters from a hammered forge,
A time for guesses, love words for the dark.

Cloudscape

Clouds coming and going, stretching, reclining, opening up a
    space
For a blue spread, a fetch of an almost sea,
    A Mediterranean in the air, and then
There is a hungry, rapacious smoke, there are hidden chimneys
    Venting their rage. There cannot be repetitions, surely never
The same sky day and night, north and south, sweet or terrible. I
    Need a brush or a Mozart horn, a serene or nearly divine
Impulse, and so there is a God up there
    Not as I thought in childhood sitting on clouds
But more majestic by keeping in balance the air,
    By simply letting be though deep in control
Of this avid air, this breath that pours out stars
    And fixes them as we travel round them. A Claude
Caught the peace, Turner divined almost every
    Mood and gesture, lashed to a mast he watched
This vast display, this ever-extending, unrepetitious act
    Of light and balance or abrupt of altering air
At which I marvel and silence myself to a stare.

Moon in December

Night and the plangent moon
　　Staring me out.
It seemed only yesterday that it shone
　　Its quarter shape of doubt.

Now it's a presence of light
　　Illuminating my room
I am glad to be a worker in the night
　　To see how it can assume

A pleasant dictatorship here
　　Over garden, square and street
In the afternoon it will be chalked up there
　　Overwhelmed by sunset.

But when the red skies give
　　Way to the early dark
I shall see that large presence of moon as if
　　It intended to light my work.

Newcomer

Say it's deceptive Spring for nights are cold,
Say it's the sun stoking its evening fires.
Say it's the sentry crocuses whose bold
Petals stand alert which makes desires
Storm me at night. I thought that growing old
Meant dignity. I blame your cunning kind
Subtle advances breaking me back to
Youth. You kindle heart and fill my mind
With love I want to show.

Aubade

A chirp, a chip in the now
Blue not total dark.
I want a music of colours
As the song begins to work
In the throat of a bird at dawn
Who unwittingly celebrates how
Sky turns bright before pale
And then the sun's full powers
As the voices of all the birds
Gather a throng of words
And give them sovereign scores.

A Music Sought

Shall I ever find
This music which I seek?
Both flutes and violins
Are scored within my mind
But something further off
I can just hear begins.
It takes both string and wind
And has to do with love

And all its thrill and drive,
Its landscape and its pace.
This music would preserve
Our best loves. They would thrive
And form a gracious dance,
Both keep our loves alive
And praise their circumstance.

Maybe no music can
Contain so deep a part
Of how we wish to live.
Both woman, child and man
Cry for the broken heart
To find a sound to give
A purpose to the hurt

We suffer and we cause.
Sometimes I hear the strings
Combine with flutes to sound
What is the best in us.
Listen, a music sings,
It's gone as soon as found,
Yet there's a universe

Which Bach and Mozart knew,
Beethoven sometimes and
Dowland often. There's
A starlight brilliance too
We but half-understand
Yet recognise as true –
The music of the spheres.

Arrival and Preparation
(Overture)

It seems to be very near
This music that's been so elusive but so quick
To offer a phrase and move into difficult silence,
Hard for me I mean.
I have let one phrase enter and disappear,
Kept only words in my mind,
But now the melody's on me at last, the clear
Psalm you don't seek but find.

Enough

A string is plucked, a word
Uttered, then silence till
A robin bleeds the snow.
Fingers are frozen, minds
Shrink to small purposes.
A thread of careful sound,
A rise of raging air
Then purpose found.

Two Together

It will always go with love, this delicate sadness,
Almost delectable sometimes as in Autumn
When the copper and gold and yellow leaves surrender
To the afterglow of Summer. I can recall
Feeling sad in September, thinking of school
And wanting the long holiday extended
For there was always love in those early days
Though it bore other names, happiness, being cared for,
Being taught to swim, being freed among the rockpools
Where I gazed at the polyps on sea-weed, smelt the salt,
And when I raised my head I saw the sun,
The noon lantern and it was almost a god.
Love took my hand when a nanny or my mother
Guided me over the shingle. Love was shining
Out of the face of the ice-cream man as he pressed
A pyramid of vanilla in a cornet.
I had known fear by night and the pain of shyness
But they were little sorrows. I must give back
The territory of love or, better, open
The secret gate to it, let others walk
In the woods of calm consolation, let the pool
Of sunlight there be waded in by them.
This I wanted to do
Even when I was small. I had no name
For the fountains of compassion cooling the heat
Of anger. Now I name and in the naming
Exorcise the terrible temper I have
Still, though it smoulders now while in my childhood
It burst out in fiery rages.

Always compassion has built its city round me
And today in a hot July I open the doors
And let a wind that's lifted an oak tree's leaves
Run round me, refresh me, offer its coolness to all.

At the Source

I was in love with someone when a child
Although I had no words for what I felt
The trust of it tamed me when I was wild,

The power of it soothed me when I had built
Dark kingdoms from my quick imagination,
Calmed me in tantrums too which were my fault

But were the other side of love. Creation
Moved me with all its falls and rises early.
I did not ask the meaning of elation

But felt it at its source where life is purely
Its own event not spoilt by man's demands
I loved and when I loved I loved entirely

And though I've tainted it and laid dark hands
Of passion and desire, in later love
I've also felt compassion's strong demands

And I have known great loves which still can move
And spring from its strong source and tell me how
There is a love which flows and is made of

My gratitude and hope, yes, even now.

Always

Always some kind of love for me, yes, always.
Sometimes a cradle-song for an older time
Or the flutes of sweetness, heralds of the Spring.

Even in childhood, the magic of love always
With nothing complete then and therefore nothing severed,
Finally love found its own right season,

Later, taking the hands of Spring, escaping
Into the Summer dances, rising in Winter
Like the cold air, the secret breath, the sighing

Of leafless trees. Places have meant love also,
Florence, Assisi, Siena, Umbria could take me
Over and opened the guide book to a much larger

City, almost a country, a state, a centre
Of the old world and the new. The voices of Rome
Rang between her hills. I climbed them all.

Love in churches, wrinkled bony women
Crouched in supplication, prayers for the dying
And the newly-born. And always they meant love

For friend, for family, always with an issue,
A new source, a pure flow, a revival,
And maybe death will be another love

Taking me through the dark forests, lighting
My way with candle stars and lantern moon
And the last words prayers of love when sorrow is

A happy sigh that's taken over by children
Calling in sweet high voices as I once did
At the start of love and before its first rich pain.

And now as Spring's a whisper in the morning
When it is nearly Valentine's loved day,
Love is the argument, the lyric moment,

The care for ritual, the need for growth
And cities rise above the misty mountains
Before the sunlight loves them with its gold.

Presences

Hard to believe in sumptuous Summer that
Dryads don't inhabit all the trees,
Nymphs stir the streams and ruffle every flat
Surface of water. Surely presences

Lived in the past when men believed in them
And danced in air and in the fiery light,
Surely spirits now provide the theme
And consolation on a humid night

If we could but believe. O credence is
All that we lack. We should be slaves to trust,
Only then will sacred presences
Guide and protect us, leap from the crowded past.

From nymph to angel is an easy move,
Cherubs turn chestnut leaves towards the sun.
Trust is the child of hopefulness and love.
A guardian seraph drives me daily on.

Friendship

If you have a secret tell it
To somebody on a train,
Somebody you won't meet
And who won't want to meet you again.
Never make demands
Or load with confidences
Possible new friends;
They deserve better than this.

They are the ones you must
Cherish and be light-hearted
At least with them at first.
They are not claimed but courted,
Honoured, considered. These
Are the one to go slow with, leave
Your tedious tragedies
Elsewhere. If you're going to love

Someone, you should take care
To notice hints of how other
These precious newcomers are.
And don't enquire of them either
Confidences which they
May want to keep from you,
In short, allow them to stay
Unused. Soon enough they will show
That they have their own way

Of making friends. Let be
Always, don't ever keep
Them on threads that are fairly free.
Why should you tie them up
Even invisibly?
They'll show you fast enough
When they want to make you free
Of their city of ease and love.

Tact is less than an art
But is a craft to learn,
And practise until you hurt
With so much discipline.
But this is the pain you must
Feel if friendship's to be
Understanding and trust,
Loving-kindness, liberty.

Total

All is and it evades me,
The trapped word, the tethered star,
The essence, almost the whole
Of me is becoming aware
Of how I have troubled power,
Dared to risk despair.
Now through five senses the soul,

The spirit of me discards crude self, takes on
Unpossessiveness.
O pure, spare moon peel off
Desire, greed, ambition,
Let me be other. Is love
The only way to this?
Even joy is a way to possess.

The full moon outstared me to show
Like it I must become less,
A sliver of self alone
Diminished to quarter moon.

Landscape and Wild Gardens

I never cared for such an ordered view.
Blenheim, Stowe, Versailles were worth no more
Than afternoons of just an hour or two.
I've always wanted wildness in the sky,
A Turner tempest and a garden where
The roses grew the way they wished. The eye

Found its own patterns. Two hours out of Rome
A garden grew in Ninfa. High above,
Norma was pitched. This was a prince's home
And I was greeted with a welcome which
Takes centuries to turn into a love
Part courtesy and part a shared and rich

Yet economic luxury. A man
Of an old English family who had
Married the prince's daughter showed me land
Where corn and nut-trees grew. Showing the last
He spoke of "The engrafted word of God"
And suddenly I saw the careful past

Of a long line of owners who also
Were stewards who must tend but not possess.
Where gardens are allowed much space to grow
And cared for quietly I've slowly come
To understand there is most happiness.
This seed was planted two hours out of Rome

When I was young, in love with Italy.
Let France and England have their landscapes made
By men who want to govern all they see,
In that wild garden thirty years ago
I learnt power means responsibility,
Gardens and poems must be free to grow

And both be ordered long and patiently.

Winter Piece

This sudden heat deludes
　　Our Winter wills and sets
Our minds on marching clouds,
　　Summer sunrise, sunsets.
We pull our mufflers off,
　　Overcoats are enough.

Then suddenly night frost
　　Stiffens our lawns and trees
And we are winter-lost,
　　Gales replace soft breeze
When shall we ever fit
　　Again sunrise, sunset?

In Such Slow Sweetness

In such slow sweetness of spirit, in such kind condescensions
Of hours and fulsome boughs, the day declines
Pasteling pale and opal skies, sharpening looks and voices.
Here's the bold bravado of almost July, here is June giving way
To everything late, hollyhocks and delphiniums,
Sweet peas and all the residents of rockeries,
Here is Summer making mankind surrender,
Wherever he can in peace,
To the pleasure of rising sap, to the laying down
Of easy flesh in the afternoon while a few
Birds bicker peacefully. We have sat still at a window
Facing West and watched the sun slip behind
Pale pink and blue and hints here and there of green.
Psalms sing in our restful minds, and near at hand
A piano allows itself to be played and its sounds
Connect our mood with what seems a kind of perfection
And echoes us back to the power of the flood-lit day.

For Melody

Such sweetness of sound, such
Melody just within
Hearing. I try to catch
The harmony, begin
A statement of life and death,
A concord in troubled years.
The trumpet demands strong breath
But the harp means tears.

Two Musics

There are two musics, one
Of human happiness,
Its pain and rapture, its joy at things well done.
But there is another utterly different which
Sings purely its own success,
Cries out of its own triumphant assertions. It is
The echo of a voice in the universe,
It knows neither joys nor fears
But takes them up and turns them into itself,
The delighted, exacting, wholly absorbing sound
Of the music of the spheres.

All that Departing

All that departing and parting
And the wounding others and lonely recrimination.
I learnt very early gifted children are many
And none is very special.
I learnt early too the pain that imagination
Can cause but its joys were vast and the time was now
And only now, it was a circular thing,
It was often a golden ring
In which my spirit danced and I was excited,
Much too excited and could not pause or sleep,
Could not stop running and jumping. It was in fairgrounds
I learnt – I only realize today –
That the flashing gilt horses, the bright blue swings woke up
     in me
The sense of the world's wonder and multitudinous
Shapes and patterns and sounds.
The hurdy-gurdy took me up to levels
Where only Mozart can carry me now, and now
Is brief and the future's on me so fast as it was not
In the sleepy leisurely moments when I lay
With my eyes closed yet watching the galloping horses,
Riding upon them, their bodies plump to my thighs,
My hands on their manes. They galloped me into the dark
Of the real dreams of sleep.

But I speak of departing and parting
And family quarrels and angry words and the hurting
Disclosures of cruel truths we cannot retract
Though we only said them in fury.
I know to the quick that each one of us is special,
Unique, particular, odd, lovable, stubborn,
Bound in the flesh and beating against barriers,
Loving the dark bodily pleasures but feeling
Always let down much later.
For I know that we all have eaten the shining apple,
Plucked it, gripped it, ruined each other with it
And yet there are transient Edens where music plays
Ineffable joys and we know that this planet is not
One among all the other orbs and stars

Rolling around the sun but piloted, ordered
By a huge spirit our little ones are part of,
A spirit which music more closely than any endeavour
Holds us to it until there is no more departing
And only sorrow for hurtings.

A Living Death

You had them all – talent, grace and luck,
Good health, fine education. You said once
Almost with guiltiness in your kind look
"When I was born I had two silver spoons
In my mouth." A book

Now thought a classic, you wrote when you were
Still in your twenties. You would go abroad
At least three times a year. Your eyes were clear
With wisdom. You could always break my mood
Of melancholy. Dear

To me you were. Our friendship was so rich,
So equal though I always felt that you
Were stronger in most things. "You've helped to teach
My mind and heart," you said. I never knew
What this could mean. With such

A friendship, so much easy give-and-take,
I'd sometimes think that you were older and
I could not bear your death. Now there's a break
I never can entirely understand.
Sometimes when I wake

Up in the night your absence fills the sky
And snuffs the stars out. You are not dead but
Have partial loss of memory and I
No longer see or hear from you, I'm shut
Away and don't know why

Except that dark possessiveness has charge
Of all your acts and words. I know you're ill
And are too early old. The gap is large
Between us, yet I hear your soft voice still.
It was a privilege

To know and to exchange a love so deep,
So undemanding, peaceful and yet full
Of wide excitement. Sometimes I still weep,
Sometimes am angry that you do not call
Or write. I am caught up

Within a death that does not die. Your will
No longer holds its former power. Your mind,
So scintillating once, has now grown dull.
There is no comfort anywhere to find
Because I love you still.

Time for the Elegy

The time for the elegy is when joy returns
And even the dead quicken at hints of Spring.
The lift of language is an art one earns

After dumb guilt and hidden suffering.
So now my memory is a room as clean
As any broom can sweep, and I can fling

The windows wide upon a Winter scene
About to alter. Blackbirds rise and sing
And snowdrops mean defiance that has been

Gathering in the quiet Winter. Spring
Sighs now, and then it stirs and spurs me too.
The dead ten years, the other lingering

In a lost memory – both of these can do
Well without me. Elegy is praise
For season and renewal and I know

Not wisdom but the wound of love now scars
And disregards them. Death as in childhood
Is not quite real but lives among the stars

Where spirits linger whose long lives were good.
Now love is round about on every side,
I hear its voices in my neighbourhood,

My doors are open and my windows wide.

Gone

Nothing of grief was said
Only there was a space in the night sky
Where a special star no longer shone, a space
Was there and made him cry
And it did not help at all if anyone said,
Who had never watched her face,
"You will get over it, others have their dead",
He did not listen, perhaps he did not hear,
The last thing he wanted was to get over it,
She was not there. One star was now unlit.

The Spirit Lifts

The spirit lifts when the skies
Lean down, lean over, and when
Scampering clouds disperse,
The moon is up in day blue
Of late afternoon hours.

You can almost become
The assent of probing light,
The assurance of accurate hours,
The day drawing together
Its cold defiant powers.

Listen, a wise man hears
An answer to long endurance
Of questions that must be answered.
The soul of such a man clears
In such high cold. He bows
To the steep honour of stars.

One Minute

Understand one minute. It's enough
And much more hard than you had ever guessed,
For when in the green shallows of our love
Did we take time to say that we were blessed?

Everything else that scarcely mattered we
Repeated over and over for pleasure's sake
Not because we thought that it might be
Not so long later, something we could break.

But break it – yes we did and gradually
As tideless waters draw back to their source
When there's a drought. Who caused it, you or me?
Who had the quick, who the abating powers?

We do not know but if we'd held on to
Just one of our best moments when we were
Not mine but yours, we might have learnt one true
Purpose when we are cold and not from fear

But from indifference or carelessness.
Lovers should cast spells or carry charms
That mark a moment which meant selflessness
When wonder drew them to each other's arms.

Young Love

My first love was all eye and stayed that way
    For months, then slowly hands
Moved to each other in a thoughtful play
    None ever understands.

O let the touch of love now for the young
    Be almost Eden – new,
We only give the darks they move among.
    Some dreadful debts are due.

The Feel of Things

The feel of things, the nap, the fringe, the sheen,
To catch the light that circles round the cat
Brushing him as you groom a horse. To show
The rueful tumble of a head of hair,
Its curl, its fall. And then there is the glow

Vermeer caught always with a modesty
Of means, a tact, a kind
Of cool respect with passion at the core,
The impulse of the mind,
While all the senses make a music of
What others feel but cannot understand.
The poem is a way of making love
Which all can share. Poets guide the lips, the hand.

Some Solitude

To be alone just as I often was
When small, before the name of solitude
Or loneliness impinged on what I did,
To be alone, my mind among the stars,
My hands brushing the lavender and herbs,
My senses clear of smoke and dirt and all
Intrusions – is this begging far too much?
Is it selfish when I go away,
Many miles sometimes,
Sometimes for only an hour when I reflect
And tilt my head to memorize the shapes
Of altering clouds in sudden heat-wave this
Whole of April offered? I think not
For in the solitude when I become
One with birdsong, shifts of winds, the slant
Of sun across the land and hill at noon
I can achieve no peace but some wise state
In which I find both pleasure and renewal,
Knowledge unknown to books, feelings unspoilt
By passion or sensation's touch. So long
As this sometimes can lead to mines the spirit
Finds its own gold in and then offers it back
To one or two or who knows what's the count,
Then there's no need to justify my purpose,
I draw away to be of use, discover
How spirit speaks to spirit, time's no matter
And none knows what amount.

Fifteen Years After a Death

Why was I hard, cruel, sullen?
Why did I turn away and want you to say you were sorry
When it was all my fault? Because I knew
You would always return, never sulk, always laugh,
Touch my hand, crack a joke, stare at me,
Never scold or upbraid me. You should have done,
You were too kind too often and sometimes brought out the worst
    in me
When I tossed real kindness to others.
Why did you never reproach me?
Now you can never touch me,
Now I am always here, now with the light on late,
Night lorries lumbering off below the window
And I am alive and wakeful and live among strangers.
The years of misery, guilt, shame, anger are over,
Good times are back but not as they once were with you
And also when I was younger.
You taught me death and I never knew you were dying
On that island in the English Channel whose name
I cannot hear spoken or even bear to see
A picture postcard of,
I was frightened, I was so much to blame.
In our childlike precarious love
You taught me that death is sitting and watching the sea
Without a smile. That is how I last saw you.
If you were here now you could learn living from me.

Legacies and Language

I have learnt my tongue
From cities that are neighbourly and near water,
Where wren or rook or sea-gull lance the air,
Where the land is flat and above it the sea sows its salt.
That was my first home,
Born in Boston, Lincolnshire,
Reared in a flat land of sugar-beet and tulips
But with mind attuned to the tides, the heart ready for journeys,
I learnt the song of storms and ships at anchor
Where the tide governs the mind. Till I was six
These were legacies but my inheritance then
Came from the damp, soft valley of Oxford's Thames
Where the air is slow and easily misted, where minds
Cogitate, think long and companionably but do not draw
Easy conclusions. For rest, for recreation,
The bells of the churches oddly ring for services
Which are not so often attended. I was a cross-breed also,
Christened to Catholic Christianity, oiled and marked
With the name of Rome on my lips. I learnt the Latin
Of stone and pillar. The Greek was soft and persuasive
But Rome spread out the glory of the Renaissance
Colours and light, huge marble presences,
Raphael's frescos filling rooms in the Vatican
And Raphael, loved by all and dying young,
Brought all Rome out to conduct him to the Pantheon.
But Rome became neighbourly when I was out of my teens
And ripe for renewal of vows. The child's belief
Had to argue with flesh and blood, must vanish, must go under-
     ground
To the catacombs and the dark long memories there
And doubt and be afraid but came up suddenly
Into the bold Baroque, into the city of artifice
Where a square is a circle, Bernini lays down his columns
And in the fountains between them and in all Rome's fountains
I learnt the sound of water, it versed and instructed me,
Took over all my English lyric sense
And gave it deeper roots and wider branches
And now, though unvisited for a number of years,
Rome does not haunt but holds me, is a presence,

Gives me a landscape utterly unlike Oxford's
And therefore a conflict that ends in the dance of phrases.
Latin and Anglo-Saxon are not estranged
But sing together as language lives and changes –
The Saxon, the Roman, the Norman, the modern with all
Its trends and touches. The dance becomes more elaborate
And carries me on and on. It is like love
That bears you beyond the guesswork of first rejoicing
And sets you on a rock facing the sea,
Your hand in another's or in the tide's or in rock-pools,
All's passionate and remote, personal yet also general,
In fact a system of rites, of comings-together
Where poetry is the common language of dreams
But also of love and its profound legislation.

The House of Words

It is a house you visit but don't stay
For long. Words leap from ledges. Verbs and nouns
Ask for a sentence where they'll fit and say

What you were unaware you thought. A dance
Of meanings happens in your head. You start
To learn a melody you half-heard once

But can't remember wholly. Now verbs sort
Themselves from nouns, and adjectives insist
You use them with great care. There is a plot

And story where the parts of speech are placed
By you and they will stay still only when
You make their purpose clear. Now you are faced

With plot and characters. There's music in
Their lives and discourse. You must set them free
By knowing where facts stop and poems begin.

For there's a truth you find in artistry
Or it finds you. The lucky words appear
And now they have a theme and history.

But you must wait a little till you hear
The sound, the tune, the undertow of song,
And now you are made suddenly aware

Of music all these words find place among.
It swoops as birds do from the living air
And nests upon your house of words to throng

With messages you never hoped to hear
And greetings which sound best when they are sung.

The Early Work

Was it there all along
   The music I seek
Now? Did a song
   Through my meanings break

In those early lines
   Of verse I made
With easy designs?
   Did every word

Find its pulse and speech
   As a thrush's do?
Now I would reach
   For the sounds and so

Discover the pure
   And untrammeled note
Which is surely the power
   Which you can't separate

From the theme. O let
   My poems find,
As stars do light,
   The music of mind.

Think Of

Think of a delicate softness. Think of a cloud,
Not what it is, vapour and air, but as
Imagination masters and names and holds it
Poised on the edge of the mind. Think of a fledgeling,
Not yet able to take the air but relying
On the thrust and impulse of parent birds. Observe
The pastel shades, the opal of going-down suns,
And the way the trees turn dark from every texture
And shade of green. Think of the shy first love
That dare not speak what it thinks it sees but waits
In a hover of happiness, not yet a depth of desire.
Think of the actual joy of a child on the seashore
Not yet divided from where he wades or how
He clings to shells or tosses them back in a rock-pool.
Think of paintings and their bold transformations,
Those portraits stilling the crowded face of a man
Or a woman gazing in a mirror. And last,
Think of the first inviting bars of a music,
The violins' first bold sweep, then the sound of horns,
And then be grateful for how the mind can dance
Between and around and under words and rejoice
And know that this is not chance.

Art and Time

It has to do with time, there is no doubt.
The clocks, the bells, the sun-dials have their power
Over the shaping of a verse. But what

The power resides in I am not quite sure.
What is certain is the way that rhyme,
Cadence and beat of syllables endure

Within the importunity of time.
Whatever form is used or if we trust
Only to ear, our stanzas cannot climb

To regions of no time. Art must exist
Within that element. Now, listen to
Any composer. You cannot untwist

His many sounds from time. Hours make them true,
Minutes absorb. And so with poetry,
Past, present, future fashion what we do,

Confine our purpose and our artistry.
And yet great verse can signal to us from
A thousand years ago. The art is free

Within the length and breadth of time. The poem,
Picture and music can be like the stars
Which flash out to our present through a gloom

Of countless light years. Yet for most of us
Time is the metronome we dread and watch,
We heed its movements and our little verse

Needs its severity, yet there's a catch
In all this argument, a wound, a flaw
Which maybe wise men could discern and touch

While makers trust to instinct, craft and more
Shapes of time they never reached before.

Pigeons Suddenly

A flight of pigeons, a sheer
Flourish and dash and delight.
Out of the pale air
They flew unexpectedly, light

And easy, graceful as
Nature is at her best.
I watched them gather and pass
And I felt language graced

And natural as the way
Birds took the air and then
Without a second's delay
Vanished. There seemed but a thin

Barrier between
Such confidence and speed
And the way poems sometimes begin
And gather force with no need

Of my intervention. Maybe
This is the absolute
At the heart of poetry,
A single ecstatic note

As Vaughan Williams found in *The Lark
Ascending*. One pure sound
Made its soaring mark
That is not sought but found.

The Luck of It

Of course it is luck in a sense,
In every sense indeed,
Lucky for you that the words arrive out of what
Really does seem a perfect, cloud-absent sky,
But the luck is not for that "I"
Which begs for sympathy, wants to tell its tale.
The poem is not your plot
Or life or worry. It is imagination
Let loose and allowed to run wild
Till it sometimes brings back a phrase or two, at times
A whole poem that needs no alteration.
What sings and tells and rhymes
Only asks that you be two impossible things
In the usual sense, that is:–
Let things be and yet be wily too
So that now and then language and music kiss
And marry and stay true.

The Start of a Story

It is so gentle as yet,
Just on the edge of my mind
And also beating quietly in my heart
But I will not say I find

A friend, not one replaced
But something itself and new
And I have no wish to own or be possessed
But find perhaps a true

New story beginning, for all
We learn to care for are
The quiet beginnings of the hint of a tale
And so there is happy fear.

Excitement, yes, but not
Much, for I feel there may be
Coming a friendship which is a love that's taught
And not demanded by me.

Against the Dark

I have lived in a time of opulent grief,
   In a place also of powers
Where self-indulgence can break your purchase on life
   But now I inhabit hours

Of careful joy and rousing gratitude.
   My spirit has learnt to play
And I have willed away the darker mood
   And now I want to say

That verse is hostile to shadows and casts you out
   When you have mourned too long.
Images always rise from the root of light
   And I must make my song

Truthful, yes, obstinate too and yet
   Open to love that takes
Language by the hand and ignores regret
   And also our heart-breaks.

Words use me. Time is a metronome
   I must keep in mind always.
Nobody really knows where poems come from
   But I believe they must praise

Even when grief is threatening, even when hope
   Seems as far as the furthest star.
Poetry uses me, I am its willing scope
   And proud practitioner.

The Sea as Metaphor

You can always use the sea
As an emblem of almost anything but, of course,
You must take the rough, the overriding white horses,
The mountains of snow tipping over and lengthening, spreading
Over the sand and through your mind. If you use
The sea as metaphor you must know about tides
And the harbour bell, the torturing rocks, the caves
Of unearthly light or else of pitiless dark,
But if you are tough and faithful, head to the wind,
Mind bobbing over the breakers, climbing the steepest,
And if you are patient with the blue calm Summer waters
Of almost quietude,
And if you will wait, then run and risk the rocks
And give the white horses their head,
You may catch the intimate, changeable rhythm of oceans,
The neutral moods which are rare, their black bad temper,
Their sudden bursts of applause.
If you are prepared to risk all this and, much harder,
Ready like patient fishermen to return
To the morning water with an empty net,
You may now and then, at other times, also catch
The ocean's rare, perfect pitch.

I Heard a Voice

What I heard was a voice
Belonging to long ago, not only my own
   Past but the past of many memories.
Classical and Romantic were forgotten,
   All categories dismissed. I heard a voice
But did not recognise it. I could not put
   An epoch or rule around it. I was myself
Uncertainty personified. In the Winter
   Landscape I fitted. In the relentless icy
Night outside I watched the stars. They seemed
   As if just scattered, released into an air
Millions of years away. And then it seemed
   That the voice I heard was vocal and no longer
Instrumental. I listened carefully and
   Heard a humming reverberation. Then
I knew it was my task to add the voice;
   Supply the language. I thought of all who ever
Practise a craft or art. It must be heard;
   Recognised and responded to. The hermetic
Obscurities belong beyond the stars.
   Art must take the hands of men and women,
Lead the children into its fastness, shut
   The door of disillusion, provide not escape
But a larger view, a danceable distance. It is
   The task of makers to lay themselves open to pain
And then cast spells on it. Only this way
   Are music, painting, poetry a part
Of the pith and nub of existence. Let there be rough
   Edges, dishevelment superficially.
But art does not copy the breakage of a world,
   Does not offer a picture of ruin or remorse
Or hand out panaceas. It speaks from the private
   Loss and grief, happiness too, it dares
To tell the truth of ecstasy and suffering
   By an alchemy no artist should bother too much
About explaining. Art brings relief, it casts
   A spell in the face of heedless stars, it works
By what one person saw and felt and endured
   As others endure. The maker is sometimes lucky

For now and then he finds the target of truth
   Not through his own accomplishment or, at least,
Only a little due to his care and crafts.
   Musical notes, visual images,
Careful words show to a few there is
   Purpose in bearing pain, but this is only
A part of sharing what one artist makes. The full
   Gift is to offer what maybe has lodged for long
In places of disapproval. Never mind that.
   I hear a voice in the watches of the night
Which one day may turn to song.

Parts

How we live by halves and quarters and
Eighths and sixteenths, never full and square
Towards a sky or season. Either hand

Is occupied, the other hangs limp where
It might have touched the grain or ringed a knob.
Babies, we crawl within a sheltered air

Watched by others but we learn the nub
And nap of things before we have the speech.
We are all concentration, fit the job

In hand, we push our limbs but cannot reach
The bear, the ball. Elders guide us from
The full experience when they start to teach

Habits, some good, some bad and so we come
At last to school and circumscription, yet
We learn to paint and take the picture home.

Our minds are filled, our memories seldom let
Our expectations down, but we exchange
The gift of self for learning score and set,

Rote and range. We can't be wild and strange
Except at night, except much later too
When love's the argument and will impinge

On all abstractions. We are full and true,
No halves or quarters then but guided straight,
Occupied fully and attain the view

Of a full moon yet it too must abate
Though it sheds gold for us and honey dew.

Let It Be

Let it be stately sometimes. Let it be sweet,
Lucid, unselfregarding, let it also
Be wholly serene and late-Summer seasonal,
Washed by the first pale suns and new-noticed moons.
Let it be ordered as hollyhock and poppy,
Scabious and columbine are in their flowering.
Let it be rich as wheat and oats and barley
Show they are, gathered up soon in swathes.
Let words of ordered rhythm sing Harvest Home
As ignorant of Winter as children are
Who have not heard of fear or seen its pale,
Close-to-death face. Death is another chapter.
Now is only the poem.

Waiting

Is it searching me out? Is the music
Playing far off? Is that what I think I hear
In December distance? A matter of horns and strings
Wait somewhere to be caught

In a mesh of words, a host of echoes, a charge
Of passion held in. Waiting is part of writing.
Poets aren't lucky to write. The good fever comes
Only fitfully while

We spend whole weeks and months with only a hint
Of a hint of music. We cannot force it, we must
Let it have its slow, sure way.

Meanwhile we live on usual levels, proceed
With little purposes, meeting, talking, not sleeping
And those nights of insomnia are not the worst to bear
Because, if they come at all,

Poems arrive in the silent small hours, seem
Part of the moon's wide definition, the stars
Shining, and so for me, sometimes for me,
And when the music begins

In my mind I always recognise the time
When it is authentic; then I leap out of bed
To grab a pencil and paper to write down the score
And of course the libretto too.

For words and their particular music are bound
Indissolubly, you must listen to both
And give them space, allow them the freedom of your
Expectant imagination.

You have to wait and then when the words arrive
At speed and racing ahead of you (that is their way
With me) then you feel that the world is indeed just
And the stars seem to shine approval.

So the lucky lyric comes and you are not sure
If there is a jarring word or a false note
So you set it aside and wait again, yes, waiting
Is the mainspring of poetry.

The Prodigal Son

He is far off, he is very far off, he's a blur
Of shadow against the setting sun, he is ragged
Clearly and slow and there is a touch of shame
And even penitence. In his vineyards his father
Is gazing at the crop, the promising early
Fruits but suddenly for no apparent reason
He lifts his torso, tilts his head and shades
His eye and something very familiar, a gesture
Of a child who has misbehaved is silhouetted
Against the bonfire blaze, "It is my son at last, at last it is
My dear lost son, my promising one, the part
Of my heart I've missed for nearly a dozen years."

In the kitchen a clatter of dishes proceeds and good
Herby smells rise up but the father is running
Fleet as a boy again and the shadow too turns
In an old and hopeless way. The boy doesn't move
For he is still a boy to his father. The sky
Is festive pink and purple. The father throws arms
About the boy and kisses the thin pinched face,
Smells the dirty clothes and a godlike but also extremely
Human compassion is seen against the light
And the boy is crying babyishly but now
Treading slowly the old good road to home
Through olive trees and herbs and the starting grapes

But in the house someone is slamming doors
And swearing and saying "It isn't fair. I was good"
And the prodigal is afraid till his father goes
And coaxes the elder son to the gala meal,
And grapes it seems have been burst across the sky.
Wine is running along the slopes of night
As a household starts to heal.

The Hours

So many hours, so many shapes and sizes, colours and arrange-
 ments, so
Many noisy, discordant ones breaking to storms but others,
 uncountable others
When the tides of the mind went out and the shore was wide and
 the sun
Shone, the moon's lamp seeming quite motionless holding
Watch over love and its promises. Listen there are
Voices praising the love of God, others suffering, monks in their
 choir-stalls keeping
The promises we have broken, uttering sorrow for our sakes, so
 much contrition
Lasting too long, so little trust. The hours
Of life turn into the sea, my ships go out on the full

And deep green tide. The hours of love return, so many kinds,
Some unrequited but no less true, some too eloquently
Demanding, the best so tranquil at times, at others almost a weeping
With thankfulness. There are drums and trumpets, there are
The limpid harp, the deep-voiced double-bass
And the boy's voice climbing to peaks we perhaps can never
Return to again though in childhood we knew them so well.

I praise now the hours of renewal and kindness and hope
When the corn is high and the apples and pears and plums
Are full and sweet. They are the harvest our imagination can
 never
Rival with paintings or poems or music though music
Sings round the planet, knows no barriers, alters
The anger of nations that starts almost always from fear.
Prime, Terce, Sext, Matins, Lauds and Vespers
And Compline that dispossesses the hearts of devils
And haunts round the patterns of stars.

Saint Augustine

Poetry always partnered philosophy
At least in your *Confessions*. Abstractions never
   Had the last word or first. Ostia improved
Upon your yearning only by being static
   And tamed down to the hour you could ignore.
'*Tolle, lege*" – you never forgot the words
   Or the order your impulses were servants to,
Gladly spying their role and quick to perform
   Their tasks. There's no discrepancy in pages
Of passionate prayer with *The City of God* you built
   Out of your mind, establishments of the heart.
Affirmed in dawn or half-light. I remember
   Seeking your mother's tomb in Sant Agostino
One Easter Saturday. I stood helpless by
   As a woman more daring and probably much more loving
Insisted the old man with his broom let us in
   "I'm writing a book called *Blood into Seed*" she told me
And Tertullian's phrase tagged the whole afternoon.
   Faint whiffs of wax and incense hung in the air
As she and I stood by in mutual reverence
   While her adolescent son stood in sullen impatience
Like Deodatus maybe entering on
   The ripe and wretched years of passion balked.
So you, my favourite saint, were present more
   Assuredly beside your mother's tomb
Even than in Old Ostia where sweet hay smells
   Like English pasture. Rome was so exact
A copy of any *City of God* since it raved
   And sang and rose from silence like the fountains,
Like your rich words in which you give to us
   Freedom of your conversion, hope in a violent age.

For Easter 1986

A violin haunts, a flute calls, recorders, then trumpets
And next, pool after pool of silence, notes falling, sounds
Dispersing. So now, this late March. So this night
Clear and cold but warmer than three weeks ago.
Easter is early, as early as possible. Must we
Catch up, count the coins, shape the wood,
Weave our crowns of thorns? In daily violence,
In loud streets, in country lanes, the crude act ruins
Itself, kills a whole childhood, nails love to splintering wood
But even so, even so,
The crocuses push up, up to life yet again insisting
On rising to drink the sun. And the blackbird carols
And cheers and rises and then is down,
All glossy feathers and yellow beak. Boys and girls
Whisper down streets, smiling, arms round each other.
Hope is there, more than desire. These are our children
Given our bleak legacy, thanking us with bold eyes.
This is a time of year and night when care
And trust and kindness rise like the prayers of children.
Some kneel at the lap of an unseen God, while others
Stand by a tree and watch the sky spread blood
Over an innocent child, over a murdered king.

Easter Vigil and Mass

It was like childhood once again but more,
More ardent and more purposeful, more realized
And possessed in mind. The Blessing of New Fire
Was all the constellations being blessed
And *Genesis* once again
And the prophecies from *Genesis* and onward
Took me back and forward yet held me still
There in the church with the covers on statues removed
And the Paschal candle the centre of the world,
Sun and moon alike.
And as the prayers continued and as I watched
The yellow flowers and golden vestments I knew
I was back in my true beginnings, baptised again
In the new water, and the church was a microcosm
Of earth and sky and there would be a rising,
Incense would bless and linger and hide the candles
Only a little, only a moment. I was
Taken up to the place where a God-made-Man
Was buried in the winding-sheets but at this Mass
He rose and came among us and we could touch him
And incense was the mist of early morning
Slowly dispersing. We walked up to the tomb
And the stone was rolled away and holy men
Told us where God was and it was good to touch him,
And then I was in a sudden childhood rapture,
The world an order within my mind and without
And held between minute and minute,
And the blood on the cross was back in the chalice, the white
Risen flesh offered to simple men,
And in the cold night underneath the stars
I felt something like love and nothing of fear
For here was holy ground and rising day
And it was right to be there.

Gloria

Is it too dark for glory?
In Winter's frozen fields it can seem so
And yet that sunset blush
Reminds of lamps that tell the Host is hidden,
Christ the child and man, the whole of God.
Glory is an object not a subject.
Little in our shabby spirits lights
Another's gloom. And yet we have known hours,
Or maybe moments only,
When... was it spirit or a heart-beat which
Stirred us to a sense of glory which
We scarcely recognised, it was so strong,
So other and so strange to usual life?
The Alps of clouds remind us of the message
That speaks of hopeful hills and sacred mountains,
Yet doubt is a quotidian shadow, tells
Our darkest purpose and our dreadful story
Which we repeat although we say we're sorry.
We should be suppliants to the turning waves,
Take the ocean's hands with gratitude,
But now and then is our best medium, we
Are fitful, changeable although we look
For love that asks for nothing, hills that tell
Of distance and can teach humility.
Listen, we're close to Christmas. Look about
For children almost innocent, for men
Who hold within their minds an ancient story.
Let us be still and silent. Thus we may
Move in the medium Glory.

In Good Time

It works in time, I think, and yet
The spirit in me often seems
To reach from flesh and hours to set
Its purpose up where poems,

Paintings and music pause also,
The soul, the spirit in each one
Of us can never ring quite false
Or not unless we've done

Such evil and dark business that
Time swings its door and we can hear
A great key turn. Is spirit what
Rings in us all most clear

And wide away from stress and mood?
In prayer and art we sometimes come
To time that tells space it is good.
Is this the spirit's home?

A Reproach

"If I believed what you do I would stay
For hours each morning and return each night"
So someone said to me, yet my thoughts stray

At Mass. My eyes drift toward the evening light
Perturbing that plain window-glass and then
I try once more to focus on the sight

Of Bread raised up and manage one "Amen".
Owning imagination, why can't I
Think of Calvary and the cruel men,

The women with no words, the men who vie
For careful, seamless cloth. I do not know.
Each week I make new resolutions, try

To think of one who made the sunset glow,
Modelled a loved face, whispered and the sea
Began to turn. I ought to be brought low

When I see Bread and Wine and can believe
They are the God-Man whom I pray to when
I want a trifling bonus for my life.

"If I believed what you do I would go
To Mass each day..." The words upbraid me still.
I who find metaphors in which to show

My poems yet strain to make an act of will
To wrench my thoughts back to the Consecration
And find it hard to say a few prayers well.

I need, in fact, a God whom I can feel
Or else remember each poem is the Real
Presence since God *creates* imagination
Which never works by any act of will.

Moving Together

Fluting voices and an azure sky
Remind, remind but all my memories
I've put in money-boxes. They're locked in
But if I wait in peace and do not try
To free them, they'll be out. A violin
Coaxes and guides me. It sings a refrain
To work of Cézanne and of Monet too.
The arts converge. *Salves* and *Hosannas*
Make a magic. Where do poems fit in?

Poets must learn from paintings. Painters keep
An eye on words but music will elude
All designs upon it. It is pure,
Tough and resistant, its own power and realm.
It holds divinity in every mood.
Beyond a mood it yet can overwhelm
The leap of spirit in us. Gratitude
Is the one refrain we can provide
As the world whispers for a hiding God.

Only

It is sad and theatrical and also it
Is going on everywhere. It means
Just changing properties and scenes,
Lowering the curtains, dimming the lit
Footlights. Of course what the play means

Alters the actions but even so
They have much in common. The chosen theme
Is love or death, fast or slow,
Possessing the quality of a dream,
Never mind where the sleepers go.

I saw it myself but of course I was
Very involved. I knew the man
Playing the lead. When the play began
I had no idea at all of the close.
It was very dark. I was part of the plan

The playwright intended, but wasn't told.
So I came on unprepared. The script
Was pat on others' tongues. I was left
Wordless, tearful, trying to hold
My own but, of course, I hadn't been briefed

Or rehearsed either. I took the call
With the others but wanted to get away
And suffer remorse alone. The day
My friend died we quarrelled and all
Was dark and wordless for months. The play

Was put on elsewhere, almost everywhere
With others playing the bereaved friend.
It took two years for the wound to mend
To leave me with the play we are
Acting daily and cannot end.

Snooker

Over the perfectly mown and rolled grass
Under a sun we cannot see they pass
Those fifteen red balls and one pink, one black,
One yellow, green and blue and brown. Arms p
A cue is chalked. This ritual we lack

Within our lives and maybe that is why
Millions watch with rapt, attentive eye
These acolytes who have such different ways
Of pocketing a red. When breaks are high
Our prayerful looks make altars of the baize.

Group Life

Observe the group life of children
As they go disregarding us on dangerous skate-board
Notice too how they break apart as from dancing
   To be other and else, wholly individual
     Yet looking out and not in

   Looking will come later
They do not know the particular pain of growing,
The senses' solitude, avaricious sensations
   They are not innocent, failure's a faint bruise
     Their scorn is directed at us.

   Time is not eloquent yet.
Let children not learn too much of punctuality
Nor fear of scolding that's almost wholly concerned
   With our abject obsession with clocks and chimes and road-signs
     Leading always to the dark.

First Six Years

I have not been back, have not returned to Boston
With its stump and sugar beet and the long garden
We played in till it became my earliest kingdom
Where my first remembered fragrance was honeysuckle,
Where I learnt of love in liftings and being cared for
Sitting in a cot, holding a little basin,
Whooping cough the first remembered illness.
And the shops where the doctor's children were always favourites,
My sister and I rushing round in small cars,
On scooters, pushing prams, plump legs to flanks
Of rocking horses. That was Day's, a shop
Huge and busy. Then there was the grocer,
Mabelson's, where rosy-cheeked Mr Mabelson
Opened bright tins and showed us new sweet biscuits,
Offered us choices. Here I learnt the kindness
That only comes in lessons of example,
Kindness again when a sister and a brother
Seeming years older than we were but probably only
Ten and twelve to your seven and my five,
They had a bright toy switchback which I longed for
And dared to ask for and they gave it me.
Never fear, never the wrong favour.
And then there was the secret, magic place,
Brenner's Bazaar where everything cost a penny,
Never a farthing more – small red tin cars, green engines, baby dolls.
They were the first treasures I stored up.
Imagination widened always longer
Than the large-back garden was and even bigger,
Then the beach at Skegness or sea at Freeston shore
My first six years were lived here. It's a marvel
Not to have any bad dreams or haunted memories,
No ghosts that rouse me sweating in the night
As they do decades later. A happy childhood –
This I had. It is the heart's first loving,
Overture to every love affair
Later, shaping, moulding and preparing.
Language was large and vivid, green as the hedges
I cut with nursery scissors. I remember
How words misunderstood are all I now

Recall of disappointment. You said proudly
"I'm going to the stations". How old was I?
Three or four. I thought of puffing engines,
The luggage on the platform, porters busy
And of course it was not this you went to but
The Stations of the Cross. My given creed
Was linked with words for signs, the Latin
"Hoc est corpus meum" later. Childhood years
And garden years and seaside holidays
Told me of God in clouds triumphant, generous.
And still there were no nightmares. I remember
No talk of sin or pain. Such debts I owe
For six perfected years, the generous hours,
The currant bushes and the loganberries,
An apple tree, a rockery, a lawn,
My parents' presences, the great arrivers
On mornings after Balls. They brought us fancies,
Favours again, gold paper crowns and streamers.
I remember now the year of the rocking horse,
My Christmas present, I rode it through all lands
Of blue skies, passed red-coated soldiers and
That day I had the first warm feel of kindness
All my own. I wished to share my gifts,
Chocolates, little toys, a first good coming
Of age and to my own well-governed country
Which never disappears from any maps,
Which we can't lose though caught in foreign traps
But that right place where, after often losing
Grace we can return to many times
And be made whole and set our precious course
Towards, and never lose the sense of homing.

A Childhood Religion

The day we invented a god
The sun was tipping the green horizon, the clouds stood still
And in our garden the hollyhocks stretched their bodies
And the strawberries swelled, the pears were hard and the apples
Shone in a splendour of light,
And out of I do not know what quick instinct we made
Our god a god of light.

Sun was his power and pleasure,
Moon was merely a thin pale copy of sun
Not to be highly regarded.
Quickly our sect seethed and gathered about it
Totem poles with eyes and knives painted on them.
Friends were forced to be initiates and
Of course there were simple tortures close at hand.

For the rest of that Summer we practised our complex code,
Our faith, our tribal customs
But one day my father took us aside and told us
"You are Christians. You shouldn't be dancing round totem poles
Or painting your faces either."
You might have supposed that our whole invented religion
Went underground then and became a subversive sect
And therefore much more powerful.
But no, we gave up the whole thing, reluctantly yes,
Yet oddly without rancour.
But that faith in a Sun God still has a niche in my mind,
Still is remembered when the Spring light turns to Summer
And the buds open, the roots stir, and the seeds
Quicken, and something quickens within me too,
A love of the sun that is close to worship, a reverence
For light whether sun or star,
And sometimes my God-made-Man seems one with this glow
And revelation beats in my heart and I think
Of the sun and the moon held in the hands of this God,
This planet entirely his province,
While his young mother hangs her head like an early snowdrop
Upheld by a host of stars.

The Essential

It will never cease, this needing, never be over.
Should it be otherwise?
Age increases but passion stays. Either lover
Or friend brightens my eyes
And as in childhood move in amazement still.
Wonder never dies.

And should not surely. Let me never become
Listless, cynical or
Uncaring about sad news of a human event.
Let me not care for size,
Even a sense of proportion can mean a want
Of love. May I not be wise

If wisdom means often standing aside or aloof,
Letting the world go on.
I care, I need, I still feel passion in love,
I tilt my face to the sun.
I cannot care for millions. Nobody can,
But from childhood I've minded the grief simply of one.
May I end then as I began.

Talking of Hume

People were talking of Hume the philosopher
Also the man who many thought was a saint,
But I was listening to his theories where
The sensuous world was held in doubt. This meant

That the writing of poetry had no purpose. So
It seemed to me. In an illusory world
Art would double the unreality, do
Away with the need. Then I heard a bold

Idea put forward, "Hume" one talker said
"Valued imagination, thought it the most
Important matter." I thought of the lyric word,

The music which takes ideas and makes them blessed.
Causality and induction disappeared
And I've learnt that Hume's ideas must be possessed.

Thinking of Descartes

I can see him cogitating, watch him with
A candle-flame. There's Descartes by himself
And by himself he's back where Aristotle,
Aquinas too began.
The crucial question is the same, "How much,
If anything, can our minds know?". The quest
Was pure and selfless, spiritual also
As any human wish can be. Descartes
Conjured a naughty spirit who might lead
The mind astray, and then he asked himself
How he could tell a dream from waking thought,
When was he sure he was awake? At last
On those pure peaks where speculation shows
Ideas can be pinned down at last, Descartes
Thought how he thought of God, a greater Being
Held in his mind, thus greater than his thought
But still the vexing query was not answered
Until, perhaps in homely and slow ways
Or, and it seems more likely, in a dazzle
Of recognition, Descartes saw that thought,
Himself a thinker, proved he was created,
Authenticated by the famous slogan
"I think therefore I am". For most of us
This is sufficient. Not for this man though.
Bravely and patiently he still pursued
The difference between the soul and matter.
He never found it but that "Cogito"
Stressed, he made clear, "I know myself,
No other". And so tonight I think
With admiration of this generous thinker,
This self-denying seeker as my mind
Swarms with what poetry is, why poems are made
And "I write poems therefore I am" won't do
Nor, though perhaps it's closer, "Poems write
Under the poet's partial power, therefore
They are." The night is warm for mid-October,
The windows open and green smells come in,
A half-moon is engaged on staring at
This little planet. I yawn and I sense

That clarity which sometimes comes before
Sleep trespasses upon us, I feel (yes,
Not think) that poems or their substance are
Upheld by moon and stars, lifted by winds
But won't be words until some poet catches
The moment and the music. I'm still back
At a beginning I've known half my life.
So maybe poems sing out the greater questions
But questions which expect the answer yes.

The Force of Time

The watch, the sundial and
Putting back the clock
Make us feel we can
Tame time but we forget
It is time's hand which mocks
Woman, child and man.

And yet in childhood we
Have to learn the hour,
We are taught to read
What clocks and sundials show
Though some abiding power
Is felt by us. We see

Seasons in the form
Of change and not of time.
Spring is winds grown calm,
Summer moods of sun
While we believe we climb
To stars by staring. Some

Memory of this
Imaginative force
Slowly fades from us
And, older, we begin
To beg time to endorse
Our little sympathies.

Maybe this is why
The great ones work with art.
One will paint the sky,
Another make sounds sing,
But time still breaks the heart
Because we're passersby

In time as well as space.
Great art lives longer than
Our lives and it surveys
The loss of time itself,
And hints immortal man
Means faith that time will cease,

That its three garments of
Present, future, past
Will one day be cast off
And we live in a power
Whose medium is trust
And undemanding love.

Of Time

Three-fold time begins
Your questing through the air,
Your ride upon the sea,
In a touched violin,
You are not three but one,
You guide us to a power
Beyond the moon and sun.

You move in one contour,
One fold of time we call
The present which moves on
And up beyond us to
The silence of a star,
And a celestial view.

Then we can listen to
Perfected music such
As drives out time and tells
In sounds of ordered touch
The purpose that we are,
But soon the angry bells

Sound in their jangling all
We guessed we were before
We heard a music small
To start with but so soon
An awesome ordered choir,
A shape of joy that tells

There is beyond us some
Spirit of lasting, and
Yes, we are sure of this,
A space that's out of time
Which Mozart makes for us
When all his meanings climb

Further than far-off stars,
He takes the best we are
Along with him until
Our spirits cannot bear
Such order and we turn
Back into time's hard will,
Its threefold turn of power.

Distractions

I settle down but not as I did when a child
After excitement in playgrounds or when rain trembled the
    windows
And I sat at the nursery table loving the noises,
Painting the sky or reading Beatrix Potter
Or simply hearing the rain like a stream of music,
Music just written by someone I'd never heard of
And didn't ask their name.
Now when I settle down to write a letter
Or lean back in a chair after hectic reading
Or walking fast, fighting a Winter wind,
I do not let silence enter me.
I cannot empty my mind.
Black thoughts of dreadful possibilities,
A parting, another death, most likely all fictions,
Fill my imagination, haunt my memory,
Padlock the past to the present and make the future
A door half open at night, swinging on wind.
All is bother and dread and untidy anticipation.
Let me learn the quiet of the evergreens,
The resilience of the robin and starling in winter,
The concentration of snowdrops, crocus or daffodil.
Take me out of myself, that cupboard that needs spring-cleaning,
And let me remember the size of the moon and search the sky for it,
Count the clusters of stars, enjoy the rain's animation,
The energy of Nature, let me now and then learn to be peaceful
And add a quiet to creation.

There is Time

There is time and only time enough. It must do
For the acts neglected, the love twisted, the children denied
Childhood and love we could not give because love
Was broken by us whenever we touched each other,
Misshapen by us when we tried to claim our rights,
For there are no rights now except the ones we've forgotten,
Simple, eager, difficult to keep shining
Though somebody polished them once.

The old are sitting by little bars of fire,
The young are noisy, dance to noise because music
We did not teach them has turned to blare and discord,
The love we failed in they seize on, grab with hunger
And afterwards turn away,
Unable to understand why they are not happy
And why they're afraid of silence.

Passion

The violence is over. They lie apart,
They are shapes belonging to no-one or could be
Part of an abstract painting or figure sliding
Upon a Dali sea.
But they are breathing fast still as if they'd been running,
Man and woman, carried by a wind blowing
Out of an open window. Here is passion
Appeased, here is pleasure
Exulted in. And here
Is possible creation. Here could be
Adam and Eve, turning away ashamed.
Here is loss waiting to be redeemed.

Mastery

From childhood I have pursued it, chased it, tumbled, picked
  myself up and then
Followed this special honour and service, this gift
That cannot be faked or fumbled for or be
Mistaken for anything but itself. It surely divides
Child and man from the animals, sets up our standard high,
Claims our right and privilege. What I admire
And mean now is mastery. For example, say,
The dance perfected, the downward swerve of the swallow,
Sure that the earth will receive it and show it off
And welcome it and try to copy it.
I speak, I suppose, of what is a kind of perfection,
Maybe the only one that we can be sure of
Here amid nondescript and shop-soiled goods,
The cliché-ridden clans and the evasive
Looks. But I've been lucky, from childhood on,
I've watched the careful gardener pruning pear trees
Or trimming trees to topiary, I've seen
The planets' patterns, the moon's inexhaustible changes
But always following through the exact advent
Of new and quarter and half and full. As a child
I lay in my bed with the door half-open and heard
Strains of Mozart telling triumph and sadness
And I could not bear such beauty but called out, begging
My parents to stop the sweet persuasive sounds
For I hadn't tears or years enough to respond
With understanding, yet maybe those young tears
I shed at the mastery of music showed
A grace much greater than any understanding
That side-steps feeling and honours the intellect
Almost too fully. Now every night of Summer,
When oak and chestnut and sycamore leaves stand still,
In breathless heat I pay my respects, I salute
The manifold masteries that man has shown
Which the child could not refute.

Energy

I have always revered it – energy leashed in
In those I love, in myself, in works of art.
It is the pith and the muscle of life, the keen
Blade of moon and sunlight, the beat in the heart

At the advent of one we love come suddenly.
Shyness is right, is part of vitality,
A holding-back before the unity
Of mind with flesh. Turner could always see

And re-create and celebrate this taut
Tension and power, like the turning-over wave
That spreads and streams along the shore. This is what

Passion exacts from tension, the rush of fraught
Tide, the turning-over wave, the proof
Of the moon's power in which all touch is caught.

Turning Inland

Inlands are always like that.
Associated with jetties
And also with estuaries which,
Being neither land nor sea,
Are a slowness, an always becoming
And never being, possessing
No name, no lasting action.
Look out, we are moving inland
Sick for the deep blue sea
And slowly learning to be

Landlubbers, returning to where
We have to belong. Each year
Turning back from September shore
I, for a time, belong nowhere,
My heart is an estuary,
My mind a pure becoming
Loving the fact of the sea
Going back to the Thames Valley where
I've learnt thirty years to be.

Resolve

I'll keep this heartbreak, let it hurt and tear
   My spirit, let it run
Through every day's best moments and appear
A joy I learnt under a happier sun.

For love so total and so simple yet
   So rich and many-sided
Is rare to know and touch, and though we're set
Apart forever now we're not divided,

Because in all mundane and brief affairs
   Rich love like this takes hold
Of future when we're separate. Let tears
Be shed. It shows me love is lithe and bold.

I mutilate the memory of you
   When I am fierce with pain
And cannot understand what broke us two,
Who were strong once, in half. But quiet again

I am the gratitude I learnt from your
   Strong mind and generous heart.
The past is our good luck, loss is no more
When I think of the love you made an art,

Friendship an act of faith. You are not well,
   Are early old and I
Must leave you elsewhere. But you've cast your spell
And left a magic which I can live by.

On the Edge of My Mind

It is on the edge of my mind, the tip of
My imagination, it is a
Theme of memory but much more. It is
A search, a ransacking, a bullying of the past,
A fight of my spirit with my spirit
But let me, let me be. I gaze out now
On a windy March four o'clock with a halfmoon already
Chalked on the sky, strangers pace by to a theme,
A rhythm not mine only my thoughts'. I am not concerned
With my childhood or first loving, but the first true flash
And demand of art, its subtle, sweet overture,
Its unceasing demands. I'm attempting now to capture
A rhythm of pure thought which must I think mean music
For I have gazed at paintings, even tried to paint
And gained only a marvel of light and confusion
Of still-lives and landscapes. Once or twice Claude
With his rapt attention, his foreground figures
Dwarfed deliberately, has sometimes seemed to answer
My purpose. It is music of the spheres,
No less than that, which will speak to my weary spirit.
No, do more, release my spirit
Till I fly like Ariel given his total freedom
But with Caliban's music singing in my ears.

Justice

It does not make you feel better
If you can write out your grief
If you can surrender to the escaping moment
Of lyrical spell-binding.
The spell soon breaks.

And why should it not? It would be
Unjust if grief could be written
Out in a facile charge. The dumb, sad many
Have no such release. Their grief and mourning are just
The same as yours or greater. Words are not sunlight
After the dark night or terrible tempest of grief.
If they were it would not be right.

Question

Would you have me turn to violent things,
The abrupt act of love, the possible war,
The intrinsic anger even in a butterfly's wings?
I've sometimes had a go at this before,

Written of birth and death and the wounds of love
And the baby weeping its hidden life away.
Yet I remember how the very play
Of art is thrilling and at one remove

Only from chaos. Surfaces I leave
Now as I watch the April Avon turn
In dark green waves as ducklings have to learn
Fresh water little tides, their brief of life.

Nocturne

This is the time for it,
This full-moon-lit night and stars and absolute silence,
This cold, sharp, defining night, this is the time
When ticks and chimes and pendula pause and I am
Simply imagination and a hand
Ready to score the music that's moving fast
In my veins and arteries. I am excitable always
In the kind small hours when I have not fallen asleep
But have become wider, fuller, more noticing, and
Now the moon and the rich deep sky surround
The walls of my mind and it becomes a globe
I fit this space and time as a perfect note
Takes hold of horn or violin or trumpet.
And now good memories are the words of a score
And I am neither creator nor listener but
An instrument that is tuned and perfectly pitched.
The theme and cadenza are childhood Christmas Eves
When I lay awake hearing sleighbells although
There wasn't even snow.
That was an act of perfect imagination
Supported, I sometimes believe, by enormous angels,
Guardian angels, potent presences.
These are about me now and turn themselves
Into kind thoughts so immediate they have not
Been filtered through memory. I remember hearing
One whom I loved telling me that I
"Had helped to educate her mind and heart"
And I never did nor even wanted to
Understand what she meant. When love's the drift
Explanations are ushered out and these
Vital, loving, guarding presences
Take me over, evoke a harmony
That can only be compared with the moments when
Love is so full it bursts through our flesh in tears,
Weepings of joy for we are needy and weak
But, now and then, are taken by very great art
Which disposes of time and holds us to itself.

A Happy Death

I

Death again but death in so friendly a fashion,
So courageous a guise that I should not weep but I do.
A man with cancer smiled at his dying for he
Knew that his spirit was moving out to whatever
Endurings there are. He wrote me a letter saying
Art was his joy, that Bach had made God his friend
And made him God's. His writing was straight and clear,
The syntax perfect, nothing at all to tell
He would die any hour. I ought to have guessed, of course,
Since he said that doctors assured him there was no cure
But he wrote serenely that he was happier than
He had ever been before. In his letter he said
That "friends mean so much and I would dearly love
To see you before I die." The letter came late
And I had been away. In the darkness I found
This white envelope with its message of friendship for me.
Early today I phoned his special number
And the line seemed to be engaged but it was not so
For when I rang the general number a kind
Voice told me that this priest had died last night.
In shock I wept and all today I have been
Close to tears and I ought to be ashamed
For this good man, a friar of fifty-seven years
Is out in the elements, one with the music of spheres
Which God plays over and over in artists' minds
For the great ones to copy out in little fragments,
Angel messages putting this frightened world
At peace with itself. But still those words "dearly love"
Move in all my thoughts, emotions and acts
Although I try to push this irony out,
What the cynic and sceptic would call this "trick of fate",
But I don't believe in fate, I trust in purpose
And also in free-will. And I ask myself
If pride is part of this grief, if what I feel
Is pity for self. The devils of doubt have come
Asking me "Is there an after-life? Can you prove it?"
I cannot but as I read that letter again
And consider it many times, I begin to see

123

The only image that man has ever conjured
That makes a little sense of all our doings.
Another ship was launched only yesterday
And out on a calm sea this man sailed for...is it
An island of the spirit? As a small child
I believed that God ruled from a throne of clouds
And what was literal then is useful now.
A breeze is up in this beautiful, learned city
Where my friend died, a city where cogitation
Is commonplace. But I remember that art
And even some of the poems which I have written
Helped this noble soul beyond acceptance,
Took him to truth that only faith can anchor.
His anchor is up and he is far away
Where salty breezes carry him on green seas
And little waves turn over. The Hours he sang
Are the songs of Syrens or sea-winds. I'll let him go,
Be glad if I can, hold back the childish tears
Until I am alone and can let them flow,
For I live in this world of violent, cruel fears
Not the one my friend must know.

II
A Letter from the Dead

I have received a letter from the dead,
A happy letter came when the tulips stand
Like Easter candles, and this letter said
Someone would "dearly love to see me" and
"Before I die" I read.

A priest of fifty-seven and my friend
Although we had not spoken for perhaps
Half-a-dozen years came to his end,
As he had wished, at Easter. Tears are traps
But sometimes they can send

Absolving waters down the cheeks. Here was
A death that this man saw as liberty
To be with God. I'm moved by so much grace
And in a tender sorrow I can see
That Christ brings living peace

To us when we are on the threshold of
Life and death. This man wrote he was now
Happy, but those words echo "dearly love".
The Easter post alas did not allow
Our meeting. Now I move

About lost in a sadness that is part
A lucid grief, an honest sorrow yet
Self is there too. Either in mind or heart
Wherever our souls rest, I feel regret
For maybe that priest thought

I needed help since he'd been near me when
My first death happened suddenly abroad
Without a warning. This man shared my pain
Without a word. Now he rests with the Lord
Who sends down such fresh rain,

Who makes the cordial April evening sky
Go red, then pink and now it's pale indeed
And a small breeze moves blossoms to a sigh.
This brave man's gone but surely knows my need
For he lives where the high

Truths and little hopes are all at one.
I learn of death but as I do I feel
Love take me over. Sweet compassion's on
My world tonight. The dead, I think, can heal
When all time's fret has gone.

III
A Song for Death

Another music now, a song for death
   Where once the dying was so brave
That I need new instruments to praise it with.
   It was a death you gave

So joyfully. You were prepared to die
   And happy in suffering as
You wrote a letter asking me if I
   Could see you. So much grace

Sang its own music from the steady hand
   Which wrote that I had been
"Much in your mind this Easter". O my friend
   If I could but begin

This week again and not have been away.
   There was no fault, I know,
But what strength it had taken you to say
   In that steady hand you'd so

Love – it was the word – to see me again
   Before you died. There is
A music in the way you bore your pain
   Such hopeful harmonies.

Is there a music in the tears I shed
   Now on this night when you
Have only left behind what we call dead,
   While your spirit's in its true

Home at last? You said that Bach told you
   That God was your friend. Indeed
Your gracious going makes music that I too
   Think of this night of need.

Need, I mean, to know there was no blame
   But only chance that I
Was an hour's journey away when your letter came.
   Let it teach me how to die.

IV

Death of a Dominican Priest at Easter

There is no waking or sleeping, no seeing, hearing or touching,
No taste, no scent and yet there must nonetheless be
Rich memories of these, deep thoughts alone at last,
Argument over and meditation only.
All at the end which delighted you now is pure,
Its own essence and nothing more. How fitting
That Bach's *Cantatas* carried you over the edge
Of living and dying to that state we in life

Come on only in prayer very rarely, in art more often, in love
That does not demand. You wrote me a graceful letter
In a scholarly hand. No-one could guess you were dying
Yet you knew you were and so did those about you.
They say you wanted to die at Easter and so
You did, my friend. You had brought God's bread to me,
Consoled me fifteen years ago when my first
Death took place and all was darkness. You said
Few words but stayed beside me and saw all
My tears. You were the kindness of understanding,
Moved by mercy. I felt the comfort in you
But something stronger also.
You wore no sign of your death but, as men of God are
Who give up their lives to becoming saints for others,
You were prepared indeed,
But you could not imagine that fifteen years on you would know
That you would be dying and utterly reconciled to it,
Totally happy. I had "been much in your thoughts
At Easter" you wrote to me a week ago,
Said, though you had "little voice, you would dearly love
To see me again before you died". You told me
It was "a privilege to have known a poet".
I hardly understand what you meant for I still
Am much in grief, touched by your truth, absolved
By your sweet acceptance. I'd been away when your letter
Arrived and told me all this. I rang the next day
But you had died only twenty-four hours before,
Gone from our senses' reach but not from our wishes.
You are awareness now and comprehension,
One with the elements. Words are so literal and
So clumsy, falling, lying, rising again.
O you have risen as music rises, you died
When all were thinking of Resurrection, when Spring
Was blithe and full and blossoms were everywhere.
Your death was beautiful, all your brothers around you.
O be my hope in your happiness. I have your letter
Full of assurance. I do not pray for you, no,
But to your spirit, one with the other saints.
O teach me how poetry must be selfless, let music
Be new in all that I write, O leave your mark;
Serene encouragement, hope in the purpose of dark.

Beginning

It is to be found half-way between sleep and waking –
A starting point, a recognition, beginning.
Think of the clouds on this planet lifted away
And the stars snapped off and the day tremendously breaking
And everything clear and absolute, the good morning
Striking the note of the day.

So it was and so it is always and still
Whether you notice or not. Forget that you are
Eyes, nose, ears but attend. So much must go on
Daily and hourly. Wait for the morning to fill
With cockcrow and petals unfolding, the round planet's power
Held in the hands of the sun.

And somewhere around are presences, always have been
Whose hands remove clouds, whose fingers prise open the sun.
Watch, learn the craft of beginning and seeing the world
Disclose itself. Take this down to a small thing, a keen
Whisper of wind, the sound of the cock or your own
Story that waits to be told.

I stood at a window once. I was four or five
And I watched the sun open the garden and spread out the grass
And heard the far choir of some blackbirds and watched blue
     flowers rise.
This was the first day for me, the planet alive
And I watched the stars' shadows grow faint and finally pass
And I could not believe my eyes.